THE NAKED RIDER

A POWERFUL GUIDE TO HELP YOU IDENTIFY, CONTROL AND CHANGE YOUR DESTRUCTIVE HORSE-RIDING HABITS

Don Campbell

www.thenakedrider.com

2

TESTIMONIALS

Having battled with riding confidence issues for many years, exacerbated by unsuitable horses, and then becoming a mum, I was about to give up on my passion for horses, and following a bad fall, became unable to hack down the road without being led. This was a paralysing fear, totally irrational, yet causing me to dismount in tears, and yet again lead the horse home.

Then I met Don on his Leadership Development Course through my job, and he offered to come and help me with my horse.

With his unique and frighteningly accurate insight into how my fears were controlling the outcome of my relationship with my horse, and his ability to identify behaviours that I was totally unaware of, Don guided me through all the complex issues I had developed.

It took time, unlimited patience from Don, and a change of horse, but now I have competed my own warmblood in British Dressage, and even though occasionally I get nervous if my horse is particularly sharp, I feel confident that I have the mental tools to take control of the situation.

I have even bought a youngster and backed him myself.

Don's approach is kind yet direct. He won't let you run away from the issue and has an extraordinary skill. I have had lessons/clinics with many well-known trainers, and I learned a lot of practical advice, but I never learned about myself, and how my mind had such an impact on my riding, my competing, and my dealings with others.

Don's methods and teachings have given me back my life with horses. I am truly grateful he didn't let me give up.

Jenny Hall BHSAI – Nurse Practitioner, Hereford

I took up riding in my late thirties; with little experience of basic lessons I didn't have much understanding of the principles and disciplines of riding. Don had a way of showing people that it started with the rider as opposed to the horse. He would look at your ability, fears, personality and how you applied it to your horse and riding. It was one of his unique qualities; I had always been taught that the problem was with the horse and not with the rider. Being dyslexic was another obstacle to overcome; I found schooling daunting. Don broke every instruction down for me so I could visually learn from it, as I struggled to understand the technical words used in schooling. He taught me that your confidence and natural ability is a great tool in riding. By applying these two elements, it gave my horse as much confidence in me as I did in him, which allowed us to work together and trust one another. Don's experience as a rider and a teacher has allowed me to be the rider that I am today. My riding experience has expanded since lessons with Don, from cross-country to dressage with a variety of horse breeds and abilities. I thank Don for his ongoing support and input and look forward to the future.

Pete Bridges – Head Chef, Llyswen, Brecon

I shall never forget our first encounter with Don. He'd agreed to help my teenage daughter with her new steed, a rather headstrong, disagreeable character. His first words I shall never forget: "Right then, let's see what you've got." Two laps around the arena and he pulled them in. "Okay, so, let's sort the rider first... then we'll look at the horse." Daughter's face was a picture!!... I just secretly smiled to myself.

And that's exactly what Don does. He sorts people and then the horse side just seems to fall into place. He has this knack of identifying the problem, and let's face it... nine times out of ten this is usually us, a.k.a. the rider... and then has this way of making us see the most simple but effective change is often all it takes.

Obviously, his immense wealth of experience, passion and overwhelming empathy for our friend the horse comes into play, but ultimately, Don Campbell is a fixer... a people fixer and one of the kindest, fairest people I have had the pleasure to meet and for whom I hold great admiration and respect. It's hard to put into few words but like so many things it all comes down to trust... trust and then when you build on the trust you get the harmony. This is what you will get with Don.

Interestingly enough, daughter holds the same opinion and couldn't wait for the next session!!

Paula Millward – BHSAI, Telford, Shropshire (typical pony club mum with a little experience under her belt)

Wow what a journey! When I think back to where I owned an almost unrideable horse, who would bolt from my rein pressure, shy away from absolutely everything, ropes included. Adding to this was the fact that he had hardly any, safe, stable manners. To where I am/we are today!

Don Campbell's timely intervention and his exceptional observation skills of people and their horses, together with his unique individual way of teaching, plus his patience when I just didn't get it! Has enabled me to look, take stock and change what was necessary in myself. Consequently these personal alterations have had an extremely positive effect on my riding, which in turn has allowed my horse to become confident, calm and trusting.

Now I ride with a smile on my face and a smile in my heart – thank you.

I truly believe that if it were not for Don Campbell's unrelenting belief in my capabilities, I would not be riding my horse today. I am sure he would have been just another field ornament!!

Francine Powell – Masseuse, Rhayader, Powys

I originally started my lessons with Don as I had lost my confidence since having my little boy. I also had my confidence knocked by some negative riding instructors.

I had not had a lesson in years; I had only ever been a happy hacker so I was also nervous about all the bad habits I had picked up.

Don was amazing from the start; he was very patient with me and made me feel really comfortable. I loved the fact that whenever I was struggling with anything he would get on the horse and show me what I was doing wrong and then show me how to correct it; I have only ever had people tell me what to do, they have never got on the horse and showed me so I have never been able to correct myself.

I would recommend Don to anyone as he has boosted my confidence so much and helped me in so many ways and made me the rider I am today.

Kirsty Rogers – Trail Ride Leader in Wales

For several years I struggled to ride properly after suffering a pelvis injury which affected my balance and hip flexibility, and subsequently had a bad fall in canter as a result. I tried several different trainers to help resolve my problems but their methods generally focused on my hands and legs and had no answer for the fear that was starting to affect me and prevented me from getting into canter. My riding just deteriorated to the point I nearly gave up completely. Then I met Don. His approach was to understand not just my physical issues but also the mental and emotional blocks I had built up towards my riding. He systematically set about breaking down those blocks, putting in place good riding practice and then piecing everything back together. As a practitioner myself dealing with mental, physical and emotional issues for others every day it was a relief to finally find someone that understood. It gave me so much confidence. I am now back riding my own horse out and finally not breaking into a cold sweat at the mention of canter, or the "C-word" as it became known!

Lisa Baker – Business Owner, Powys

CONTENTS

CHAPTER 1
"USE YOUR BRAIN NOT YOUR REIN"

Brawn against brain... but who is using which?!

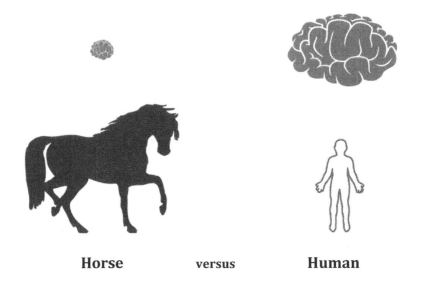

Horse   versus   **Human**

Think about the above relation between the horse brain and the human brain in terms of size and capability. Then look at the physical dimensions between the horse and us humans.

The horse brain is about the size of a large walnut whilst the human brain is about the size of a melon. The horse's weight is 500 to 600 kilos on average, whilst the average human weight is approximately 65 to 85 kilos.

If you look at the common sense of the pictures it is obvious to see what part of our anatomy we as riders should use the most. So **WHY** do so many riders try and use physical strength and force against their horse? It seems obvious when you stand back and look that the physical size is a real mismatch; there is no way you can win in a physical contest.

The human brain, however, in proportion to the horse's is so much larger and better equipped to solve some of the simple problems that the horse presents you with. Yet at times you are easily outwitted by your horse as they push you into their area of expertise, and the next thing you know you are in a physical battle against your horse. Your horse has caused you to have an instinctive emotional reaction which can last for a moment or for a lot longer. Your heart feels anxiety or fear and your brain and logic switch off so your mind becomes fogged and you can't think so you react and just GRAB to try and survive. Sometimes the reaction is a simple slight tightening of the reins and a firming up of the leg, or it can be an all-out grab of the reins and a total overreaction to the situation because you are fearful you will lose control. All of this happens in a split second; how fast you get back the control is down to training, personal growth and development.

You are trying to maintain stability and balance between your **heart**, which is full of emotions, and your **mind**, which is logic and control over the ability to handle yourself physically and apply the riding that is required at that moment in time.

Notes

Notes

Notes

CHAPTER 2
"KNOW AND CONTROL YOURSELF FIRST, THEN
LEAD AND INFLUENCE YOUR HORSE"

Winning my heart and mind

The purpose of this chapter of *The Naked Rider* is to put the book in context for you. Please do not worry; I am not going to ask you to "strip" and ride naked, as I can tell you from personal experience it really chafes your vulnerable parts. That said however, if you do want to try naked riding, first of all pick a sunny warm day, and use a saddle pad NOT a conventional saddle as the stirrup leathers really nip your lower leg, and never ever ever do rising trot!

That's not to say that at times during the reading of this book you will not feel vulnerable, because I suspect at times you will feel a little "naked" and vulnerable, so what I want to do for you here is give you the right "aims and expectations" for both the book and for yourself. This is a book to help horses with their people problems. Together you and I are going to change the world of the horse, one person at a time, starting with you.

The book is about you. It's about your personal leadership of yourself and your practical leadership of your horse. It will also focus on the most important part of your leadership, and that is you and your relationship between you and your horse.

So what is leadership? Leadership is "winning the heart and mind of ourselves and others to achieve a common purpose or common goal". This includes the heart and mind of your horse.

We win hearts by first winning trust, respect and confidence; we do that by generating feelings. We generate feelings of excitement, challenge commitment, ownership. We find and create a sense of pride in what we are doing and what we are trying to achieve. We create a sense of pride in ourselves, our appearance, in our horse, in the way we ride, in the way we school, in the way we treat our horse and other people. It is this pride that is the central motivation of all of us.

We win the minds by being clear and concise, by providing a framework and structure to work within; we give ourselves clear goals and boundaries for those goals. We make ourselves very clear of what we need to do, how we need to do it and very importantly **why** we need to do it. The reason to be clear in our own minds is so we can be much more focused; we can then see if we transgress off of our goals and make the necessary adjustments to our thinking and actions to come back in line with the goals we have set. These goals can be on a large scale and/or a day-to-day scale. On the large scale you might set a goal in dressage of competing in a prelim or getting to compete at a Grand Prix by the end of the year, or doing a clear round or competing at an open 140-cm in showjumping or doing a cross-country round at a local venue to competing at your first British Eventing 3-star. Your large goals don't need to be at competition, but they do need to be realistic and attainable. They also have to "stretch" you a bit, and they need to have a realistic timescale; but set the goals you must. You then need to do the day-to-day work to stay on track, so you also need to set day-to-day goals to check you are still on course for your larger-scale ambitions.

For example: I used to go into the schooling arena and school my horse and sometimes I would have a good session and sometimes a not-so-good session, but always I went in and "did schooling stuff". It was only when I started to set myself goals for my sessions that I was able to measure how successful my training sessions were. It was only when I started to set the goal of riding straight down the centre line, or getting the walk to canter on the first stride, or cantering for four strides and trotting for four and then cantering for four strides, that I was able to measure myself and my horse against my goals. Before I decided to set goals I would only feel whether the session was OK or not... now I can measure that and make adjustments to me and my horses' training accordingly.

What we are looking for is success. That success is for both us and our horse. Our own personal success can be measured against the goals we set. Our horse, however, will measure success in their terms, not ours. Our horse will measure success in how it affects their life in the here and now, because horses live in the moment, not in the future. It is the little pat on the neck, or the scratch of the withers; it's the words of "good boy", the kind tone in our voice, the gentleness in our riding, the feeling that our horse gets when we love them in the moment. This is how our horse measures success.

It does not matter if the success we are looking for is in competition or success out on a hack by achieving going past something we are scared of, or success in a schooling session; it is this chance of success that drives us on and success is that harsh criteria on which we are judged. That judging will come from our horse, if we listen, as well as other people, but more importantly it will come from ourselves. We need to have success as it is this that grows our confidence; the more success the more confident we become, but we must never become overconfident or arrogant as "pride comes before a fall". Success, and even lack of it, is key to our future growth and development. If we succeed we must pull the benefits out of that success so we can replicate it. If we have a lack of success, we need to analyse it and work on a way of improving.

All development starts with us. It starts with us winning our own heart and mind first; it starts with us being able to lead ourselves first. For if we lack confidence or we feel inadequate, if we are confused with what we are trying to do or achieve, if we are unclear in any way, we are going to fail. If we cannot give of our best and finest in creating the success we want then we will not get, nor indeed should we expect to get, the best and finest from our horse.

The starting and finishing point for all your riding and personal growth is:

"To know and control yourself first, so you may then control and enable yourself and your horse to perform at the highest level of competency."

You cannot control yourself until you know yourself; you need to know your strengths, weaknesses, vulnerabilities and needs. You need to find out what are appropriate behaviours, and what are inappropriate behaviours. You need to find out what switches you and your horse on, what switches you and your horse off. You need to know how you affect your horse and indeed how your horse affects you. You normally only find all these things out in testing situations; you don't know how you and your horse will react "under fire" and pressure until you both have been "under fire" and pressure. This might be in competition, cross-country or showjumping or even just walking out if that is a particular challenge for you. Once you know how you and your horse are affected then you can start to make decisions on how best to apply that knowledge to create the success you want.

You will make mistakes, that is a given. The greater the mistakes, believe me, the greater the impact of the learning. I once drove 56 miles to a dressage test. I had all the tack loaded, polished and cleaned, nice shiny boots and very white jodhpurs, and a little bit of complacency as I had done it all before. I decided to pack the lorry very early in the morning instead of the night before as I was a bit tired that evening. Big mistake! I arrived at the show, I got dressed, opened the tack locker, then opened the back of the lorry and had the shock of my life: I had not put my horse on! I am now never complacent; I pack the night before and do a checklist and last on the list is... horse, check!

For that learning to be effective the learning has to be self-evident; only you can change your own attitudes and behaviours, and you can only do that if first of all you are aware there is a need to change and you have the inner determination, commitment and self-control to make the changes that are necessary.

It is vitally important therefore that after each ride, after each schooling session or even after you try for a specific movement from your horse you review what you have done. You need to be able to review by giving yourself and seeking from others, open, honest, constructive feedback. A simple review structure might be to start with a one-word "feeling" after you have schooled that sums up what it was like for you; were you pleased, happy, disappointed, angry, excited and so on. Then explore why you were feeling the way you did, what was causing you to feel that way. For example if you felt "happy" was it because you did something right or your horse did something right? Then work out what "right thing" it was that you or your horse did. If the feeling was negative and maybe you felt disappointed, explore what it was that caused your disappointment. Don't just go all sulky about it, try and get to the root cause of what was going wrong. Once you have this information work out a way to replicate the good things so you can feel happy more often, and eradicate the negative things. Learning comes from both good and bad feelings and it is important to look at the good feelings as well as the not-so-good feelings.

Once you have explored your feelings and worked out what

you are going to do, move on to the next part of reviewing your session: that is to write down the "Good Points". Write down what is was that was really good. Was it how you applied an aid for example, was it your attitude that was good, was it the way your horse responded to a specific aid, was it that you tried something different and it worked? Whatever the good point was explore WHY it was so good and WHAT made it good specifically, then very importantly work out what you need to do next time to replicate that good outcome; I don't mean in general terms, I mean specifically what ACTIONS are you going to apply. After you have done this start to look at "Improvement Areas". Again write down specifically the prime areas you want to improve on next time; it might be a softer hand, a more still hand, a firmer leg, a more accurate circle and so on... Once you have written the improvement points down look for the one that is the single most important one that you really want to do something about. It might even be a combination of several of them, but try and distil down to one "Key Action Point". When you have it, take that Action Point along with your Good Points into your next schooling session and be fantastic!

For all this to be effective you need to keep an open and enquiring mind, not by instantly accepting or rejecting what you and others may say but by at least being open to the feedback you and they are saying to you. Be open to the feedback even if you hear something you disagree with. For example, I may tell you that you are not helping yourself or your horse by wobbling about on top whilst trying to keep your balance, and that you would benefit in getting some exercise to strengthen your core stability and get a lot fitter, because you get very tired part way through your lesson which makes for sloppy riding and that does not help you or your horse get any better! Don't dismiss it because it is a bit painful and it might be difficult to accept; put it on what I call the "mental shelf" where it can rest and sit for a moment whilst you maybe calm down a little! Then later on when you are in a better frame of mind and maybe a little more relaxed, take the feedback that was a bit painful down off the shelf and look at it with a bit more objectivity; there may well be some absolute gold in what has been said and you just need to sift the learning out once the emotion has subsided. If you don't find any learning in what has been said then don't discard the feedback, just put it back on the shelf and store it as it may come in useful at another or more appropriate time.

As you progress on through the book you will be asked to do some work sessions. It is important that you are as honest and as open as you can be. You may find some things out about yourself that you don't know both on the negative and positive sides of you. If you find something you don't like about yourself please don't go into a depression and think you are worthless and useless. Use this knowledge to spur yourself on to change it, make it better, make you better. If you find a real positive that you really didn't think you had, don't dismiss it or feel embarrassed and get all coy about this very real addition to your strengths. Embrace it, nurture it and make it even stronger.

You spend so much time, money, effort and energy trying to control, develop and grow your horse, that you often forget the second part of the relationship... **you**... the human part in our equine/human relationship.

The Naked Rider is going to give you the power to control, develop and grow yourself by helping you turn the energy and effort you normally exert outwards towards your horses, inwards towards your own personal growth so you can become the rider your horse has always wanted... and so they can become the horse you always knew they could be.

It doesn't matter what level you ride at, whether you are a happy hacker, Olympic rider or any and everything in between. We all carry thoughts and emotions that have an influence on us and our horse. These thoughts and emotions more often than not dictate our actions and behaviours. Some of these actions and behaviours will be positive and good, whilst some will be negative and downright destructive to ourselves and the relationship we are trying to generate and create with our equine partners.

You cannot stop yourself thinking and feeling, and these thoughts and feelings will change from moment to moment. For example: when I am at a dressage competition and going through my test in my mind I am on top of the world, focused on my dressage test and confident. Then suddenly as I go through my test in my head I can't think of the next movement at "B", so panic and fluster starts to set in and my confidence takes a dip. I then take some deep breaths, relax, calm down quietly, and think, reread the test and I remember what the movement at "B" was and apart from relief I am back on top of the world again with my confidence back to full strength. All this happens in the space of a couple of minutes.

The key part is to use these thoughts and feelings in an intelligent and constructive way so you become master of them and not a slave at the mercy of them.

To do this you need to first of all have an awareness of them and an understanding of your reaction to the thoughts and emotions that are generated. For example: if you are frightened, how do you act? Do you run away (flight), not get on your horse, just do ground work, but for all the wrong reasons as they are excuses and you are just avoiding and running away? **"If you turn and run, you will only stumble and fall."** Alternatively, do you get into "battle mode" (fight) where you get on your horse no matter what, and become over-brave with what you are doing and push your horse beyond their and your capability? You are aggressive and even brutal, because you do not want to be seen as a coward either by others or by you. If you do this you are then a danger to yourself and your horse and you are an accident waiting to happen. Also, the damage you can do to your relationship and trust with your horse can take a long time to repair. Fight and flight are at opposite ends of our reactive scale, and if we look at the behaviours between the fight and flight we will be able to take very different actions; if we can get our thinking and brains into gear we can decide in a very conscious way how we will deal with the situation we are in. If our tendency is to run away when we are over-challenged then we need to maybe just stand still for a moment, breathe, control our urge to panic and run. Switch your brain on, start to try and think logically whilst standing still and stopped.

If our tendency is to "draw our sword" and go into battle mode and fight whatever challenge is put in front of us, maybe we need to take a step back from the "overexcitement" of it all and again get our brains into gear, calm down, steady the rush of blood and open our eyes and minds to other possibilities.

When you turn your thinking on and engage your brain you will be amazed at how many options you create to get to the same place, and with much less stress all round. Especially to you and your horse.

Here is a very personal example of when I was torn between "fight and flight": a couple of years ago I had a very bad fall. I was thrown off a horse on to a fence, having been thrown over the horse's head from a violent buck after a rear. I twisted in mid-air to land face down, from a height of about 10 feet, horizontally on the fence around my arena with both of my legs striking the fence about three inches above the knee. I saw (in slow motion) both of my legs invert and bend the wrong way. The pain was so great I thought I had broken both heads off of my femurs. As I lay there feeling faint and sick, I started to regain some feeling in my feet and lower legs and was able, after about an hour, to move both of my lower legs. I realised my legs were not broken. However, I had done some very serious damage to the ligaments in both knees, especially my right knee which had landed on a fence post with such force that it split the post.

Consequently I had to have open surgery on my right knee. Some 12 pins, bolts and staples were used to hold it all together and in place, to reconstruct my knee. After some four months of physio, gym work and stretching exercises, which at times were very challenging to say the least, it was time to start riding again!

Between the accident and up to the surgery I was still riding my horses. My right leg was very unstable from the knee down, to the point I occasionally staggered to the right as if I were a bit drunk. It didn't seem to affect my riding too much with most of my horses. However, one horse in particular, Lap Dancer, is very sharp and is quite a hot little number; she found that I had a weakness in my right lower leg and decided to test it. She would wait until we were in canter and after four to five strides she spun her quarters against my right leg to the outside and then stop dead; I would then fall off on the inside, which is her left. Falling off once could have been put down as being unfortunate; however, she did this three times with me over a period of a week on three separate schooling sessions in almost the same place with exactly the same result: me coming off. So I decided to not ride her until my knee was sorted after surgery.

So it is now some four months after I have had the surgery. I have done the physio and gym work, and I was feeling good and needed to ride a horse again. Lap Dancer had not been ridden for four months and I really wanted to ride her as she would be my greatest test. I put my jodhpurs, boots and half chaps on and tacked her up as I had done hundreds of times before. I took her into the school to the mounting block where she stood beautifully still for me. Then it started: my internal emotions were running an absolute riot. I was scared, excited, anxious, nervous, worried and I felt incredibly vulnerable at the same time. Self-doubt crept in: could I still ride, would she let me get on her back, would my knee hold up, will my knee be strong enough if she throws in a buck or a spin? My confidence was ebbing and flowing like a tide. I was bouncing internally from fight (just get on and to hell with the consequences) to flight (just take her back to the stables and let someone else get on her first).

I really had to sort myself out; take some deep breaths, calm myself down and practise what I preach. I stood there for some 20 minutes to try and balance my internal emotions and get a grip on myself so I did not keep "pinging" from one extreme to the other. Eventually after a lot of indecision, my mind became clear and my heart became calm. So I gave her a pat, said good girl, put my foot in the stirrup and my other leg over her back and into the other stirrup. My heart was in my mouth but I kept my breathing regular and steady; I calmed myself internally and used internal talk to reassure myself of my own confidence and competence. I used external talk to Lap Dancer to reassure her that all was fine; this also had the effect of keeping my mind focused on Lap Dancer and what we were doing. I then quietly asked for walk then trot; we warmed up for about 20 minutes. My knee was holding up; it felt a little sore but that was to be expected. Lap Dancer was great and my confidence grew. I still, however, had one more thing to do and that was to ask her to canter. I knew that this was the key challenge for me, so I put my leg back, softened my inside rein and asked her to canter, and into canter we went. Five strides later she spun her quarters... I didn't budge, and my lower leg didn't give way. I am not sure who was more shocked at me not coming off, Lap Dancer or me. My confidence grew again, and so did hers; we were back together as a partnership, trust had been restored for both of us. She has never tested me in that way again!

Out of this came some huge personal growth for me as my default in these types of situations is to go straight to "fight" and battle my way through; "fortune favours the brave" and all that! This however, has taught me there are far more options available to you when you open your mind and listen, and the key is to find a way that works for you when you are in the heat of battle; that is the battle inside yourself and not the external battle.

It is your instinctive reaction of flight or fight which starts to play inside that dictates what you do, and from that moment on you are at the mercy of instinctive actions. Whether they are good or bad doesn't matter. It's the fact that you are not in control of them that stops your choices and decisions. Instinct cuts off your thinking as it is an emotional charging of your body and mind to either fight or flight for survival.

This is at its rawest and deepest level. Most of the time, hopefully, you are not riding in a survival situation.

However, the instinctive reactions can still be seen (even when it is not about survival), but in a more sophisticated way so you are still not the master of your own destiny; you are at the mercy of your thoughts and feelings.

The start point to changing this is awareness: to be aware of the internal thoughts and feelings that are causing external actions and behaviours, then having the power to change them if needed.

Notes

Notes

Notes

Notes

CHAPTER 3
"YOU THINK YOU ARE DOING EVERYTHING RIGHT – BUT YOU'RE PROBABLY NOT"

Self-awareness

Self-awareness is the starting point for all the other enabling factors to improve your performance. Whether you are on horseback, on the ground, or even teaching and instructing, without self-awareness you can go nowhere. You stagnate. If you do not have self-awareness you can only react to circumstances. **"Without self-awareness, we probably think we are still doing everything right."**

The awareness you need to have is an awareness of an insight and an outsight: to be aware of what is happening inside us to the reaction and responses on the outside in our horse and their behaviour. You then need to fit the insight to the outsight and connect them together to be able to see reality as it is and not as it is perceived. For example, you might be feeling nervous as you approach a particular cross-country fence and you are very aware of your nerves (insight); your horse, however, is "perceived" by you as going forward because that is what you really want to happen in your mind, when suddenly as you get closer to the fence you are aware your horse is backing off from the fence (outsight). Now you have to connect the two parts together and take some appropriate action before it's too late and you both come to grief.

To be able to get this reality, you need to be able to stand back almost like a third party, so you don't delude yourself with a false view. This is a really hard thing to do as you are of course part of the problem you have created. This said, you are the only solution.

Once you have this reality, you can then start to draw the right conclusions about the situation and change or confirm your actions for a better or sustained outcome.

Out on a hack you see the gravel bin "with teeth" of course, and your anxiety comes up because "he always spooks at gravel bins". You are not at the bin yet but your internal emotions (insight) are already starting to dictate an external reaction (outsight). You become a little tense, you ride differently, a little more defensively maybe. You might just tighten your seat a little, take a slightly firmer contact, press a little harder in the stirrup. Your horse can feel every tiny little anxious movement. Then, all of a sudden, "spook" and off he goes – that little soft-shoe shuffle he does that catches you totally unaware. And you were concentrating so hard and putting so much effort in to your reins, and legs, and balance, and seat, you then say, "See, I told you he always spooks at grit bins; he just knows it upsets me." No one can convince you that you are the problem and your horse is not the problem. Worst of all, "He does it on purpose!" This gives your horse way too much credit for cognitive processes he just does not possess.

The above is an example of a real situation I was coaching; I could not convince the lady she was causing the issue because she was anxious. So, I decided the lady rider and I should swap horses. My horse has been along this road a thousand times, he lives here, and really is bombproof. He doesn't spook at anything. I rode this lady's horse, and the first time past the bin her horse looked, but walked on, and didn't even look at the bin a second time around. However, to my absolute surprise my "bombproof" boy was shying and snorting at the bin! The lady was shocked to realise it was her that was causing him to spook. This proved beyond any doubt to my lady pupil that she was the problem and not her horse, who she said "always spooks at grit bins and he does it on purpose just to upset me!"

From that simple example, you can see that if you used self-awareness, the reality of the problem is not the grit bin; it's the rider's anxiety. So the start point for a solution is totally wrong as the rider is focusing on their horse and not themselves. So they are then going to exert external control of the horse instead of what they should really do, and that is to exert internal self-control over themselves and their anxiety.

Once you have that good level of self-awareness, you can really start to look at what you need to do to increase your self-control. You cannot tell your feelings what to feel as they are going to feel them anyway. What you can do though, if you have a good level of self-awareness, is start to choose what you do when you feel them by increasing your level of self-control so you can affect more consciously your subconscious behaviours and actions. If, for example, you are aware of the physical tightening of your hands on the reins or closing your leg a bit harder or stopping breathing when you are frightened or anxious; you can bring the fear and anxiety into your conscious awareness, as the fear and anxiety are the cause of your external behaviour. So if you calm yourself, deal with and manage the fear and anxiety internally, you can then physically do something about softening the reins, you can breathe more slowly, you can relax your seat and leg; you can then change the outcome.

Your horse might still spook at the grit bin, but at least it won't be because of your anxiety. It will be because the grit bin really does have teeth!

Now you need to start your journey.

Make a list of the 5 things in your riding that you know you need to improve:

1

2

3

4

5

Now pick one item from your list for you to work on and really concentrate on what it is you need to **do** to improve it (outsight).

Now put the two things together – the item and what you are going to **do** – and turn your insight and outsight into a reality and make it happen.

Once you are progressing with that one, pick another one and focus on that one, then another and so on. Then start another list and keep doing this for the rest of your life so you continually grow and develop as a rider.

Now list the 5 things **within** yourself you need to improve to become a better rider:

1

2

3

4

5

Now pick one item from your list for you to work on and really concentrate on what it is you need to **do** to improve it (outsight).

Once you are progressing with that one, pick another one and focus on that one, then another and so on. Then start another list and keep doing this for the rest of your life so you continually grow and develop as a person.

Notes

Notes

Notes

CHAPTER 4
"USE FEAR TO SHARPEN YOUR COURAGE, NOT BLUNT YOUR SPIRIT"

How we learn

There are two main routes to learning and both are important. They are called the Intellectual Route and the Emotional Learning Curve. We often have a preference for either the intellectual or emotional route as a start point for our learning and development. This can often be situation-dependent, but we often have a deep-seated feel as to which one we would rather start with.

Some of us start by going down the Intellectual Route where we read up on a subject and do some studying about it before we try anything, whereas others would travel the emotional route as our primary, and just get on and have a go to see what happens and then work it out from there. There is no right or wrong, just a preference at this stage.

These are the **head** and **heart** routes to learning, and you need both to be able to succeed.

Too much head (Intellectual Route) and not enough heart (Emotional Learning Curve) means you keep on gathering information to the point where you don't do anything. You get into analysis paralysis and never apply the information.

Too much heart (Emotional Learning Curve) and not enough head (Intellectual Route) and you become too "gung-ho" with no applied thought until after the event, when often it will be too late. You are excited by the experience and forget to think.

The key is to know which one you need to "beef up" on in

relation to the situation you are confronted with. You are then able to create a balance within your growth and development so that you "do what you know, and know what you do".

Graphically explained below are the Intellectual Route and the Emotional Learning Curve:

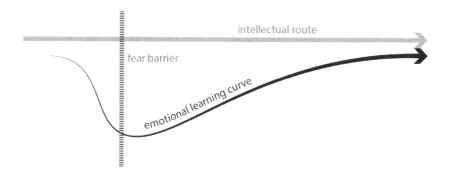

As you can see the Intellectual Route is a straight line. You are gathering information and intellectual understanding without any form of physical application of what you have learned.

If I use an example of the Intellectual Route in teaching my four-year-old son to ride a bicycle for the first time, I might start by first of all explaining to him how to ride a bike.

"Well, son, here is your bike. As you can clearly see it has two wheels, one on the front and one on the back and these are attached to a frame. Also on the frame is a saddle which you sit on, and handlebars, at the front, that you hold on to and this is what enables you to steer around corners. Attached to the handlebars are two callipers called brake handles. You apply pressure to them with your finger grip; this then tightens the cable which is attached to two other callipers that squeeze brake pads against the rims of the wheels which will slow you down to an eventual stop. Be careful not to squeeze too hard on the front brake as this will lock the front wheel and you might go over the handlebars.

"You will also notice a big cog in the middle of the frame with two offset pedals on it and a chain attached going to a smaller cog on the back wheel; this is the forward propulsion system."

I then take some time and explain all about the dynamics of balance. Then I tell him what he needs to do: "You sit on the saddle, hold on to the handlebars and apply alternate downward pressure to the pedals. This then creates forward momentum and off you go."

What a splendid job we have done on the Intellectual Route. My four-year-old can now ride his bike! Of course he can't.

On the other hand, I could teach my four-year-old son to ride his bike by going down the Emotional Learning Curve first. In this scenario, both he and I are very excited and just want to get on with it. So we go to a small hill, I sit him on the bike, give him a push and yippee off he goes! For about five yards, and then, crash, bang, wallop, off he comes and face-plants into the tarmac. So this route doesn't work on its own either.

We need both routes for success. All information (Intellectual Route) with no action (Emotional Learning Curve) means we don't DO anything. All action (Emotional

Learning Curve) without information (Intellectual Route) is foolhardy and sometimes dangerous.

I could use both routes to teach my son to ride by just curbing his excitement (Emotional Learning Curve) a little and giving him enough information (Intellectual Route) to keep him safe. I hold on to the back of the saddle to support him whilst he works out what he needs to do in applying (Emotional Learning Curve) the information (Intellectual Route) I have given him.

As you travel down the Emotional Learning Curve it is rarely a smooth ride. The feelings of excitement, thrill, anticipation and exhilaration can very quickly turn when you fall off to anxiety, anger (at people and stupid bikes), and you can start to blame and dump the problem on to other things and other people. You start to feel fear and a loss of confidence when you are at the bottom of the curve. At this point you start to choose whether you are going to press on to the other side of the fear line or go back up the curve to where you perceive it to be safe. If you go back up the curve and stay there you will stagnate and not progress. However, the fear of going forward can cause you to freeze.

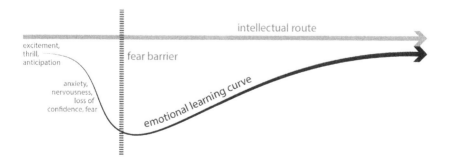

How you now deal with these emotions and the situation is absolutely key to your success in the future. You need to understand what has happened and to do that you need to use and look at both the Head and the Heart.

The Intellectual Route (Head) is your "black-and-white" unemotional, logical, detached part that allows you to analyse and scrutinise the factual information.

The Emotional Route (Heart) is your sensory system that enables you to survive. It is your external antenna on the world around you that gives you your whole internal spectrum of feelings. If these emotions and feelings get blocked, your whole progress stops dead. If you become consumed by anger or paralysed by the fear then your energy goes into externally attacking and/or blaming other people and things for your lack of success.

Or indeed you can start to beat yourself up and confirm you are useless and no good. And boy, can some of you do this well!

What you need to do is turn that energy towards yourself and positively work out what you need to do to sort the problem and push up against the Fear Barrier and then through it. I am not saying it is easy, but what I am saying is it is necessary to develop and grow and move forward.

On the other side of the Fear Barrier you get your first small taste of success and this is so exhilarating even if it is tiny. It is still a success, and with this comes a huge change in your confidence.

You start to believe in yourself. As you push further along the Emotional Route you start to feel you can cope, your mind opens to further information and you then start to look at possibilities.

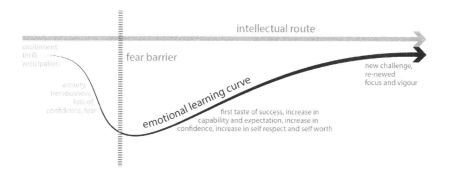

You open up a whole different future of challenge and stimulation where you are the deciding factor of how far you grow and develop.

You are not held back or held down by negative internal emotions and destructive internal voices when you lose confidence that tell you, "You are no good," and "You can't do that."

You start to become "master of your own destiny".

Notes

Notes

Notes

CHAPTER 5
"IF YOU FEED A POSITIVE OR A
NEGATIVE – IT WINS"

Internal voices

We all have internal voices. Some are kind to you and confirm what you have done well, whilst other voices beat you up and are very negative and destructive. Some voices tell you the truth, some tell you lies, and some delude you with false realities by telling you that you are better or worse than you actually are.

You have all sorts of different voices in your head from your past experiences and past people to current experiences and current people. All of these will have some form of influence on the way you feel about yourself and that will inevitably influence your attitude, behaviour and actions, which will ultimately influence your performance.

Filtering the information from these voices is quite a task as they all have some form of relevance and credibility. Sometimes they might confirm your fears whilst other times they challenge you to be more courageous. They might confirm you are useless and rubbish and start to knock your confidence they say things like, "I knew you weren't any good at that; I don't know why you even bother," or "I think you should just give up." They might say something like, "Go on, do it. You know you can; give it your best shot, at least have a go," and push you to build your confidence. How many times have you said to yourself "I am going to enter that dressage/showjumping/eventing competition," and then not gone? The internal voices have told you, "you or your horse are not ready," so you "bottle" out.

Whatever these voices say you must not let them dictate your behaviours and actions without you being in control. They will constantly chatter away at you, especially when things go wrong. For example, you may have ducked out of a jump because you thought it was a bit too high and you were scared or you thought your horse was too strong. You were on the wrong stride or, for whatever the reason that you come up with, the fact is you didn't do the jump.

Now the voices start, and you can hear them if you listen. They say things like "You chicken," "You wuss," "You shouldn't even be on a horse." Or they might say, "Well sat, as you knew it was too high," or "Well handled, especially with your horse being that strong: nobody would have tried it." These voices can have the effect of either knocking you down and keeping you there all depressed and despondent or building you up to have another go. The key part is to listen to them first and to then take control of what they are doing to you. The voices seem to have more credibility after some form of action or experience as they are very "wise in hindsight".

This is when you are at your most vulnerable to their influence, and if you are not careful the voices will dictate an action that you will not be in control of.

The information was available to you before you ever got near the jump but you, for whatever reason, didn't have the confidence to listen. It was this that stopped you making the decision in foresight.

Sometimes you might be too excited at the beginning to hear them. So you can't or don't hear the positive side of your internal "chatterboxes" to help you see the reality of a situation and make better judgements and decisions. At the beginning, the voices might have been saying, "The jump is too high," or "Your horse is too strong," but you didn't hear them. Afterwards however, when it has all gone wrong, they really start to make themselves heard by beating you up especially when you say to yourself, "I knew it was too high," or "I knew I shouldn't have done it." Then you give credence to the voices to really go for it and kick the living crap out of you!

If you can start to listen to these voices early enough, and sift the truth from the lies, you can see a clearer reality and start to make better decisions. If the voice says, "The jump is too high, you can't do it," there is both truth and lie in the statement and you can choose which course of action to take. The jump may well be too high, so you could lower it and build up to the height. The "you can't do it" may well spike your courage or competence; it lays down a challenge that you might need to look at and not be reactive to. You need to be very aware of not just what the voices say but what they cause you to feel and do, so you are much better prepared mentally and emotionally to make and then take a better decision and a more positive action based on truth and reality.

You must not let these voices either hold you back or, indeed, drive you off a cliff. You should listen to them and allow them to have the right influence on your actions where you are in control of what that action is.

These voices can have a devastating effect on your confidence when they are negative. You don't need other people to beat you up and give you a hard time as you can do a much better job of that on yourself! Don't let the voices do it; tell them to STOP.

Find balance within yourself; look for the things and words that build you rather than destroy you. Be positive, be clear, be kind to yourself and be forgiving of yourself. We all make mistakes; they are what help you grow. Use the mistakes and voices to grow and develop you and not to destroy you. If you make a mistake, look at it, take away the learning and move on. Don't sit and wallow in the negative that surrounds it!

Listen to the positive and the negative, then blend them together so you have more of a balanced view. Both will have some credibility and both will have some validity. How you feel often dictates which one you give the higher credence to. Too much negative destroys your confidence; too much positive can delude you and make you arrogant.

So always take a balanced view before you decide which one to give more credence to.

Notes

Notes

Notes

CHAPTER 6
"BEWARE: EXCUSES ARE ALWAYS
FEASIBLE AND PLAUSIBLE"

External excuses

"External excuses are where you blame other things, other people, or other problems for your lack of performance."

Excuses are often used to avoid looking at the real problem, which is often an internal feeling of incompetence, inadequacy, stupidity, fear, anxiety, nerves and many others. These feelings often embarrass you, and as a consequence you can feel diminished in some way, so you find external excuses to save face and dump the problem on.

If, for example, you are anxious or frightened about a jump or nervous about a competition you can start to dump your problem on all sorts of things. For example, your horse "doesn't feel right" or "the saddle feels loose" or "the horse feels non-responsive in this bit" (which happens to be the same bit he is always in).

Other places to dump are that you "have a bad knee, back, shoulder" or "didn't sleep well". This can go right down to "that person over there is laughing" (it must be at me, is what you are really saying, and they don't even know you). You are hypersensitive to every little thing.

You are very good at finding excuses that other people can't quantify or qualify away. All you are doing is running away from the real problem and not facing or confronting the internal issue and sorting yourself out.

More often than not it takes far greater courage to admit and face the fact that you are frightened, scared, nervous or anxious than it does to face the jump or competition. "If you turn and run, you will only stumble and fall."

You need to give yourself permission to feel what you feel and not make external excuses for your lack of courage in facing the issue. You need to take personal responsibility to turn and face your inner fear. Then you can start to work out a progressive movement forward, bit by bit, to manage the fear in a more positive way. The way to manage fear is with courage. **"There is no courage without fear."** The fear may never go away, but at least it does not have to control you and make you freeze up and miss out on all the fantastic experiences that are on offer but for external excuses!

A person I teach used to always say they didn't "feel right" when I asked them to canter their horse. There was always something: they would suddenly feel nauseous; they would be too tired; their legs felt like jelly because they had trotted for too long; they hadn't slept well; right through to their horse really didn't feel like they wanted to canter today!

They even said to me they couldn't remember the aids for canter and would start reciting the most complex set of hand, seat, leg and weight aid movements (that a contortionist would have difficulty in doing) to check out with me, and to try and get me to confirm that indeed they couldn't remember how to get their horse into canter. They were trying to make me complicit in their problem. Then, of course, they started to blame me in not teaching them the proper aids for canter.

After the lesson when they were standing on the ground and their horse was in the stable I asked them for the canter aids and they reeled them off perfectly without any hesitation. So I then asked why they couldn't remember them when they were on the horse. After a bit of questioning and gentle persuasion, they said they were scared.

This was the breakthrough. Once they admitted they had a problem, which was that they were "scared", we could work on the real solution and not be stuck in excuse after excuse. I asked what they were scared of and it was the horse, as they had seen the horse gallop in the field at play and it looked really fast. They were frightened they would not be able to control or handle the horse as it looked very scary.

The start point to their improvement in riding was an admittance of what was causing the real problem, and in their case it was fear and a lack of being in control. So the lessons went on a very different path. We worked on confidence and control of fear. Some work was on horseback and some work was on the ground. They stopped running away from themselves and this enabled them to build up over the course of a year the courage, competence and confidence to not only canter in the school but to go out and canter in open country under control.

They still had some anxiety and nerves, but they managed them in a way that allowed them to improve their performance. So, don't make external excuses and dish out blame on to other things and other people. Face yourself and work out the real issue, then start to tackle it... bit by bit!

Make a list of the five most recent external excuses you have used that have stopped you doing something with your horse or riding:

1

2

3

4

5

Now, look at the excuses, and write down what you need to **do** to stop yourself using these excuses.

1

2

3

4

5

Now that you have the solutions, do not just let this be an "Intellectual Route" exercise. Make sure you **do** the work on the "Emotional Learning Curve" and apply the solution.

Then each time you slip and use another external excuse, come back to this exercise and start the solution again. Don't stop trying and don't stop applying solutions.

Notes

Notes

Notes

CHAPTER 7

"DISCOVER THE POWER OF STILLNESS"

Calm

What is calm? Calm is an inner state where you are aware of all your thoughts and emotions at this moment in time and none of them are dictating your behaviours or actions. You are still, within yourself, yet able to move of your own free will if you choose to. You feel at peace with yourself and the world around you.

Each one of us has a different calm. We each need to search and find from within what that calm means and how we manifest and create it. To create calm, first of all you need to be consciously aware that calm is missing from you and is needed. Once you are aware of this you can then decide to create your own calm. First, still yourself, breathe, listen to your heartbeat, find silence and shut out the "white noise" and clutter of sound from around you; find the place inside yourself where only you can be, and go where you feel safe and at peace with your world.

For some of you, the picture and feelings of calm might be blue skies and sunshine. For others, it might be the crashing waves of the sea or a storm and high winds. It might be the stars on a frosty night or a warm humid tropical night with a soft breeze. It doesn't matter what or where you find the picture of your calm. What matters is that it is your own version of stillness within you. It is not nothingness, for it has a purpose to allow your thoughts and feelings to become one so you create balance within and are then able to deal with the situation of maybe what put you outside of your calmness.

A good place to practise is while you are off your horse's back to start with. Then, when you start to get better at finding your calm, you can then transfer the experience whilst on horseback. This will enable you to see a better reality of what is happening on the outside of you and connect that with what is going on inside yourself. This will then enable calm and help you choose a more effective path for yourself and your horse.

Some simple things to ask yourself:

- Do I hold my breath when I am not calm?

- Remember to breathe. It is a basic of life, yet many forget to do it when on horseback except when the instructor says, "Breathe!"

- Do I fill silence with clutter and chatter?

- This is a good self-created distraction to stop you finding a calm place, so you "talk, talk, talk". It stops you having to deal with yourself and listen. "STOP, LOOK, LISTEN... BREATHE."

- Open your ears not your mouth. Listen to the sounds and voices outside and inside you, hear them in your calm world... then choose what to do.

- Do I blame others for my lack of calm? Do I dump it on my horse or my instructor?

- Take responsibility for your own thoughts, emotions and actions. Whilst external influences and actions may well have a dramatic effect on you, don't blame them for your inability to stay calm. You have to take ownership and get control back over yourself and your situation. Whilst you are busy blaming, you are not calming.

Find the reason you are not calm within. When you do, do not stop there. Find a solution rather than just an affirmation of a reason.

We find many reasons not to be calm, especially with our busy, busy, lives, and they are nearly all excuses to not put the hard work into ourselves. Don't get distracted; do the work on your inner calm and that will pay dividends on your outer behaviour and performance.

Make a list of the five things that affect your calmness in a **POSITIVE** way. Things you can create and recreate in your mind.

1

2

3

4

5

Practise going to these places and being in a state of calmness. Find the time to be there and go to these places for just a few minutes every day. You will find benefits in all areas of your life, but especially when you are schooling your horse as that is where (within the context of this book) you will find it of huge benefit.

Notes

Notes

Notes

CHAPTER 8
"PRIDE COMES BEFORE A FALL. ARE YOU OVER-CONFIDENT OR UNDER-CONFIDENT?"

Self-confidence

Self-confidence comes from success and achievement: the success of succeeding; the success of winning; the success of picking up challenges (no matter how big or small). All of these things grow and enhance our confidence. Self-confidence also comes from the knowledge and experience that you can cope and handle yourself in the situations that confront you. Self-confidence is the wellspring inside you that allows you to release and use all of your natural talents and abilities.

That confidence is often fragile and is easily dented. When you lose confidence your capability, knowledge and thinking often floats straight out of the window. You find it difficult to think and/or do anything. You can start to panic on one hand and do and take inappropriate decisions. You might decide to do a higher jump than is necessary just to try and bolster up your fragile confidence; you know all the time it is the wrong decision but you just can't stop yourself, and because your internal motive is wrong for putting up a higher jump the chances of a success is really in the lap of the gods and not in your own hands. You can run around like a confused headless chicken. You say things like "Shall I put the jump up?... shall I not?... or shall I?... or shall I just do flat work?... or go for a hack?..." Or you can freeze and become like a rabbit trapped in the headlights of a vehicle so you just groom and clean tack!

You then start to beat yourself up and the internal voices

84

start to say things like, "I knew I was no good. I knew I couldn't do it." You get on a downward spiral of negative emotions and destructive self-talk. This needs to **STOP**. **Stop** beating yourself up, **stop** confirming you have lost confidence, **stop** putting yourself down. **Stop** giving other people permission to confirm you are not very good by telling them that you are "not very good", and then trying to get them to agree and be complicit in beating you up mentally and emotionally. What you do is say things like, "I really didn't get that right, **did I**?" and you set other people up to say, "Well it wasn't very good." Then you say, "I knew it, I was total rubbish." By saying that, you then set them up again by being even more negative about yourself. They, being a good friend, may well say, "Well, it wasn't that bad," to try and stop you knocking yourself even more, and that gives you the opportunity to dismiss them by saying, "You're only saying that because you're my friend," and so it goes on. The confirmation to yourself that you are not good enough and your confidence takes a dive... again!

It's time to change all that negative behaviour and **START** to take a more positive and constructive approach. **Start** thinking about what you do right. **Start** thinking about what you do well. **Start** to put things in perspective, because **sometimes** you get it wrong **NOT** always. **Start** to be far more positive about yourself.

Riding a horse probably has the greatest effect of all when it comes to building or diminishing your confidence. The horse can do fantastic things one minute and make you feel like a champion. Whilst a stride later, your horse can make you feel devastated and you start to think you should take up knitting as a hobby. When your confidence takes a knock, for whatever reason, you need to refocus and concentrate on what you do well and rebuild from a more solid base.

Go back to when you were confident with your riding, even if that was a walk. Give yourself permission to be pleased with your decision and start to rebuild your confidence from a firmer footing. Give yourself permission to restart something and not just press on and on in the vain hope that it will come right. I see so many people spend forty minutes fighting and battling their horse and ten minutes at the end getting it right. Then the next time it starts all over again – except the ten minutes at the end becomes eight minutes; then six; then... Well, you get the point. To the horse **all** training is learning. Your horse has no differentiation between right or wrong. You have just spent forty minutes building up the best muscles for your horse to go into battle with you next time. So the forty minutes' battle is what they learn because that is what you have taught your horse. You have taught your horse how to make you unconfident and eventually you give up because you do not want to get into the fight yet again!

Start with the ten minutes at the end and it is a totally different story. You don't have to have the confidence-sapping battle. Do something that you and your horse can do well; rebuild your confidence in each other at the same time. Then gently and quietly increase your demands of one another. If it goes wrong, don't get destroyed by it. Go back and start again.

Also, don't get pushed around by other people; don't let other people make you overstretch your confidence. Don't let other people keep you down either by keeping you doing things well within your capability because they don't want you to outshine them. Don't let other people knock you down and be negative. Get rid of negative knock-you-down people. Find and surround yourself with positive people who want to grow themselves and help you grow at the same time.

Now, it's time to do some work. List the five things in your riding where you are at your most confident.

1

2

3

4

5

Now go out and practise these five things. Don't get complacent. **Perfect practice makes perfect.** However, be kind to yourself and if perfect doesn't happen, don't get cross or despondent. Try again.

Now list the five **who** or **what** knocks your confidence.

1

2

3

4

5

Now start to get that or them **out** of your life. Make some decisions about the people around you. Make some decisions about your instructor.

Get an instructor who takes you into consideration and pushes you to become a better rider and a better person by encouraging you and not being negative and knocking of you. Find an instructor who is enthusiastic and positive and wants you to succeed. Find an instructor who demands from you and of you and doesn't pull punches, but doesn't beat you up either. Find an instructor who has a sense of humour as well who will laugh with you and not at you.

Even make some decisions about your horse: you might be over-horsed or under-horsed. Yes, I know it can be difficult, but maybe your horse needs to be made happy with someone else and you need to move on to a brighter new future with a new partner.

Ask yourself whether you push yourself enough or too much. Do you overdo it and have unrealistic expectations, or do you just stay well within your comfort zone?

Answer all the above questions and write the answers down on the blank "notes pages" and then **action** them. Don't let the answers sit as an intellectual exercise: **do** something about them. Continue to have success and grow your confidence. If you have a failure don't get despondent; use that failure as a massive learning opportunity.

Notes

Notes

Notes

CHAPTER 9

"CONCENTRATE: AND JUST BE BRILLIANT"

Strengths and weaknesses

We all have strengths and weaknesses; these are the straws that create the bricks of who we are. You have mental, emotional and physical strengths as well as mental, emotional and physical weaknesses. Your strengths have a very powerful upside; they have an equally powerful downside too. The upside and the downside of your strengths and weaknesses will manifest themselves in either positive or negative external behaviour. What you need to learn to do is turn on your strengths and positive behaviour whilst you handle and control the weaknesses and negative behaviour.

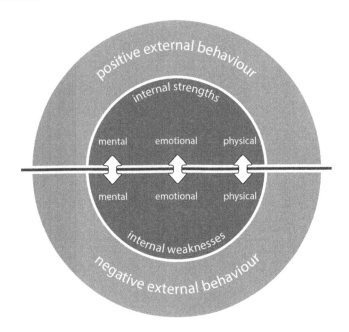

For example, you may well have the "emotional strength" of sensitivity. This makes you very sensitive to other people's feelings and what they are going through. You are very good at reading people, so often you can be kind and caring to them because you understand their emotions. This strength is also shown when you are on horseback as you are sensitive to what is going on with your horse and you are able to shape your riding accordingly. You are often told you are a sensitive rider. This is a very powerful upside and the behaviour exhibited is very positive. However, the downside of your sensitivity is you are so oversensitive within yourself.

You don't take criticism very well, if at all, and the slightest negative towards you can often lead to you lashing out at other people. If, after sensitively riding your horse and really trying hard they are still not being or doing what you want, you can often lash out at them too. Maybe you give them a "jab" in the mouth or an over-strong kick in the ribs or a sharper crack on the hind with the whip.

After you have lashed out, you then feel guilty for what you have done or been and desperately try and make up for it. You make up for it with people by over-apologising and/or buying little presents as a sign of how sorry you are. With your horse, you give them an extra feed or a few more carrots. With the people you might get away with an apology and small present. Your horse, on the other hand, doesn't understand that a few extra cuddles and carrots are an apology!

You might have the "physical strength" of a strong seat, strong core and lower leg whilst riding. This gives you good stability, it keeps you and your horse together and you are often seen as a strong rider. All this is a very powerful upside. The downside, however, might be that if you have to ride a more sensitive horse you might be very stable in your seat but you could overuse the leg and fire the poor beast into the middle of the next county as your obvious strength suddenly flips over and becomes a weakness.

You may well have the "mental strength" of creativity. The upside of this is you are great at coming up with new ideas and ways to do things. If you hit a problem in your schooling, you can really get creative with all the different ways you could change the situation. The downside can often be that you are so creative you never make a decision as to which idea would be best to use, so you vacillate and become indecisive.

The key part of having the information about your strengths and weaknesses is to be able to, on one hand, use all the positive behaviour and understand your strengths, whilst on the other hand you control and handle your weaknesses and negative behaviour. The start point for you to be able to do this is to find out what your strengths are, then to look at them and turn them on consciously so you are fully aware when they are working and aware when they are about to work against you.

You will notice that I have not asked you to write down or look at your weaknesses. This is for a very good reason. I really want you to concentrate on using all of your strengths and positive behaviour. What I want you to do is to so concentrate on being brilliant so that the weaknesses fade into minor moments of insignificance.

I want you and your horse to focus on what you do really well and push each other to ever greater strengths and positive behaviours so that your experience of riding becomes ever more positive for you both.

Now it's hard-work time again. Write down the key five strengths for each of the Mental, Emotional and Physical Headings.

Mental

1

2

3

4

5

Emotional

1

2

3

4

5

Physical

1

2

3

4

5

Now look hard at these points and realise these are very positive things about you. These are some of your talents that you should be very proud of. Now find an example where each of your strengths has been used to a great and successful outcome. Now look at how you can apply that strength more often. If we concentrate on using our talents and abilities, we will not have to try and improve our weaknesses and feel vulnerable so much. I am not saying we should not try and improve our weaknesses; what I am saying is to keep them in perspective. The improvement of our weaknesses is not the only way to grow. The enhancement of our strengths and talents is a far more positive way to grow.

Now you have a better understanding of your strengths and the positive behaviour they create, I want you to look at the flip side to them. Write down how and when your strength becomes a negative to you. Then I want you to look really hard at HOW you could have maybe stopped or adjusted yourself to keep the positive behaviour going and limit the negative behaviour that may have taken away what you wanted to achieve at that moment. This will give you some key indicators for the next time; it will increase your awareness of when it starts to be wrong. Now you have a chance to do something different before it all gets in a tangle.

Create a more positive atmosphere around yourself. Find positive people to be with. Find an instructor who gives you praise for things you do well, as well as correcting those things you don't do so well, but in a positive and caring way, that makes you really want to not let yourself or your instructor down. So both you and your instructor raise your level of expectation of performance.

Find a professional or a star that you admire and would like to ride like. Look at how they ride, look at their habits, skills, subtleties and try to emulate and copy some of them. You will, of course, have your own way of translating what they do to graft the skill on to your own so that it becomes yours and this can then be added to your strengths.

Don't be threatened by people who are better than you; be inspired to be better. Get rid of negative people who have a detrimental effect on you and always knock you down or hold you back... You don't need them!

Notes

Notes

Notes

Notes

CHAPTER 10
"LOOK IN THE MIRROR; IT'S WHERE
ALL YOUR SOLUTIONS LIE"

Improving performance

Improving performance is achieved by the **practical application** of change. It is not improved just by reading up on a subject as that only increases your knowledge; it is not improved just by discussion with others as again that only increases your awareness and knowledge. Until you have put into practice the increase of awareness or the new knowledge, your performance will not and cannot improve. You have to practicably apply something, to DO something in reality. You have to take the increase of knowledge and awareness and apply it in a practicable way that creates the change you need to improve your performance. For example if you read up on how to do a shoulder-in you will have increased your intellectual knowledge. In your mind you have already done the perfect shoulder-in, just like it said in the book; however, in reality your actual performance will not have improved until you are on your horse and applying your new-found knowledge in a practicable way. Then you will find out if you have improved your performance... or not!

These practical applications may at times be so subtle that only you yourself will see or feel the difference and the improvement in the performance because the changes may be very personal. You might just not feel as frightened or as nervous as you used to because of something you have adjusted in your attitude and thinking, and the only person who really knows that is YOU.

In the context of this book, the performance we are trying to improve is of course you, your horse, and your riding. There are two main components you are dealing with: you, "the rider", and of course your "horse". What will happen is you will have what is called the RIDER APPROACH and that will elicit or cause a HORSE RESPONSE.

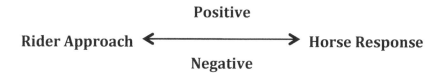

Positive

Rider Approach ◄—————————► **Horse Response**

Negative

What you are looking for is what you the rider did that caused a positive response from your horse, and what you the rider did that caused a negative response from your horse. You are also looking at your horse's response to your rider approach. Was your horse's response positive or was your horse's response negative? Did it then cause a change in your rider approach? Did you adjust your approach in light of your horse's response or did you just plough on with the same aids looking for a different reaction? The rider's approach and the horse's response is a constant dynamic between the horse and the rider. The reading of response and approach is what gives you the information to change. You can then apply that information in a practical way and improve the performance of both you and your horse.

As riders and instructors, or even as friends and observers, you need to try and develop the art of looking from the outside into yourself and other people and, of course, **your horse**. Then you need to try and understand the internal cause of the external behaviour. You can only change from the inside. The external behaviours are easier to see as they are more on display. However, it is the inner cause and inner attitudes of the external behaviour that need to be addressed, changed or improved.

For example: your horse may be heavy in your hand. So you attack the problem from the **Horse Response** and you decide to use a stronger bit because "that will back him off and make him lighter". After a little while, you end up with the same problem of the horse being heavy in your hand, so you go for an even stronger bit, and then stronger and so on, until you don't know what to do.

Now let us look at this in a different way using the **Rider Approach** to affect the **Horse Response. You** may be too heavy in the hand and hanging on to the reins and that causes the horse to respond in a heavy way. How can a horse possibly be heavy in the hand if you are not hanging on to the reins?

The question to ask is: WHY is the rider hanging on to the reins and being so heavy in the hand? It could be because they are nervous or scared of being out of control or falling off; it could be they are very unbalanced, or indeed any number of other things. The key part is that it may well not be the horse, so putting a stronger bit in the horse's mouth probably won't change any of the real reasons as to why the horse is heavy in the hand. However, if you work on the rider and get them/you to be less nervous and less scared, work more on balance or whatever the **real** problem is, you will then have a change in the "Rider Approach". This would then change the "Horse Response". You can only change yourself: nobody can do it for you. When you are aware there is a need to change and you persevere and make the necessary changes within yourself, then you will get an improved performance.

It can sometimes be very easy to say that it's your horse that is "the problem". Riders say to me in lessons, "He won't do it," when they ask for something from their horse. The rider then tries to solve the problem from the horse response end by asking louder or harder or crosser. So I say to them **stop**. "If I get on, do you think he will do it for me?" More often than not, the riders reply to me by saying, "OK, so it's not him. But I can't work out what to do!" It is sometimes too easy to DUMP on our horse as after all they can't answer back in an eloquent verbal manner, but they do answer back and well we know it!

The true way to start to listen and hear what your horse is telling you is to ask yourself key questions whilst you are riding:

- "What am I feeling?"
- "What am I feeling from my horse?"
- "What is the cause of those feelings?"

If your responses to these questions are positive ones, then ask yourself, "What did I do to cause that?" and very importantly, "How do I recreate it?" Practically and physically, what is it I need to do so I can have that positive response and positive feeling more often both for myself and my horse?

If the responses to these questions are negative ones, then again ask yourself, "What did I do to cause that?" and what do I need to change to stop the same negative feelings happening again to both myself and my horse?

Having done all of the intellectual work of working out and thinking about what to do and what not to do, now comes the exciting bit: putting into PRACTICE the changes you need to make. It's the practical application of these changes you want to make to both yourself and the way you ride that will improve you and your horse's performance.

Write down the five things you want to improve about your horse's performance:

1

2

3

4

5

Now write down the five things you are going to change in YOURSELF (rider approach) to improve the performance of your horse (horse response).

1

2

3

4

5

Now take that step and start your own personal journey.

Notes

Notes

Notes

THE AUTHOR

Don believes that "at the root of every horse problem there is a people/rider issue" and he approaches training from that perspective. Don believes that horses, like people, are the same yet uniquely different, so training and development **MUST** be tailored to the individual horse and the individual rider. Whilst the exercise, jump or movement may be the same, the application and the learning will be specific and unique.

Don is a leadership development specialist and for 26 years has worked with and helped many chief executives, senior directors and managers of both large and medium-size companies in improving their personal leadership. It is his huge experience with people and their personality and character traits, as well as his passion for horses, that he brings to his training.

Don took up riding as an 18-year-old training point-to-pointers, which is relatively late in life, but has been a passionate rider in all disciplines ever since. On his first day at the racing yard, he had his first lesson on his first ever ride. This lesson was one sentence long: just as he was approaching the gallops, he was told, "If you get into trouble, stand up in the saddle." That was sound advice at the time! Later that day, he had his second point-to-point lesson: jumping. The advice was given *AFTER* his first jump, which ended up with Don's face meeting the horse's head over the jump, resulting in a bloodied nose and broken tooth. The advice was: "Oh, and put your head to one side."

Don is a single parent to his 13-year-old daughter Molly and his 22-year-old son Calum. Molly is a very talented rider and already knows she wants to be an international competitor in dressage! Calum loves a different kind of horsepower... cars!

Don can be contacted by e-mail:
don.campbell@thenakedrider.com

Lightning Source UK Ltd.
Milton Keynes UK
UKOW06f1253090516

273858UK00001B/177/P